The Divorce Toolbox

Surviving the Courts, CAFCASS and Social Services, while Leading a Normal Life

By

Mayapee Chowdhury

First published in Great Britain in 2014

© Mayapee Chowdhury 2014
ISBN: 978-1-910115-30-5

Prepared for Publication by LionheART Publishing
House

For my family, who never give up on me.

Contents

Introduction

In 2008 my life changed forever: after a long-haul journey, I gave birth to a beautiful baby girl. Three weeks later I left my husband and took a life-changing decision to divorce him. Two major changes in my life all at once: not just a new mother but a newly divorced single mother. Since then my life has been a journey of courts, an organisation called Children And Family Court Advisory and Support Service (CAFCASS), and social services; you name it I've been there. My character has been assassinated to the maximum and I've been accused of everything under the sun. I have survived and I am still standing. In this book I will not only tell you about the journey I've taken but be your travel companion on your own journey.

Throughout this whole process I have learned a lot and there is so much that I didn't know at the time, but which I am wiser to now. We are all human and prone to getting it wrong; you need to be a saint not to. During the course of my proceedings I've also discovered how not to do things, from both sides. There are times when I've made wrong judgement calls and let the stress of the whole situation get to me, to the point of losing my cool. Never feel disheartened – all is not lost. I will guide you through how to redeem yourself if you do make an error of judgement.

I am at the point now where other people in my same situation are asking me for advice. This has inspired me to write this book, to pass down my pearls of wisdom and give you the survival tools to deal with the trials and tribulations of this whole process. Above all I do not want people to suffer in silence and feel as if they don't have a choice.

On this journey there will be practical and emotional matters to take care of. Whether you're in the process of making the decision or have already done so, this book will guide you. I have split the book into sections, which can be read in order, or you can read the parts that are relevant to you and dip in and out as you feel is appropriate.

I will be covering practical matters such as taking care of finances, preparing for court cases and vital interviews and, most importantly, how to look after your own health and wellbeing.

Please be aware all cases are different and this book is not a substitute for proper legal advice. This book is based on my experience of my own case as well as others that people close to me are happy for me to share. I will use some of these examples to illustrate the points I am trying to make. For legal reasons, however, I am not at liberty to divulge too many of the specific details of my or other people's cases. Each case is looked at on its own merits, so please do seek expert advice.

Chapter 1 – To Divorce Or Not To Divorce?

I will not impose my own personal views in this chapter but will go through how I finally reached a decision. For six years I stayed in an abusive relationship, until I ended my marriage when my daughter was three weeks old. In the six years of my marriage many attempts were made to reconcile, including counselling. Like many, I was also under the delusion that a child would change our marriage. It did, but not in the way I expected.

During my years as a married woman, I tried to justify to myself why I should remain in the relationship.

<u>Family And Society</u>
Your decision to divorce should never be based on what your family, friends or society think. People who genuinely care about you will stand by you and not judge you. If they do not then that is a sign that you need to detach yourself from them. In many Asian communities there is the fear of being ostracised from society. Ask yourself this question:

'What is more important: my and my child's safety and wellbeing, or society?'

The more extreme question to ask yourself is:

'Do I want to be excluded from society, or be beaten up, or worse still cut my life short?'

Everyone knows which option I chose; otherwise I would not have lived to write this book.

During my divorce, some family and friends stood by me, but unfortunately others not only turned their backs on me, but used my situation to ridicule me. I have not only cut these people out of my life, but I have gone on to meet better people and enrich my life.

Ending Up Alone
If you are afraid of ending up alone or of the loss of your married status, ask yourself this:

'Isn't it better to be alone and happy?'

I felt lonelier when I was married than I do now. I know a lot of single people who are happier than married people.
   If these are your fears, they are not strong enough reasons to not do it. Someone very wise once gave me this piece of advice:

'When you lose friends you can make new ones, when you lose money you can get it back. When you lose time it's gone forever.'

Financial
If you are staying in your marriage because you are relying on your husband's income, there is good news. You do not need his income to survive; there is abundant

help and support out there. This experience could be the making of you, giving you the opportunity to pursue your own career and make your own money.

One of my financial reasons for staying was that I wanted to please my parents as they had paid for a lavish wedding; money they could have used to cover other expenses. At the time I divorced, my father was about to retire and my mother was looking for part-time work. If they had not spent so much on a wasted celebration they could have enjoyed a better or even earlier retirement. They did not look at it like that, however, as they got a beautiful granddaughter out of it and saw me live longer and happier than I otherwise would have, had I stayed in the marriage.

When it comes to making your decision, be selective about whom you discuss it with. You also need to be very decisive and act quickly, especially where there are children involved in very hostile circumstances. In these situations, the sooner you make the decision and involve a solicitor, the sooner you and your child are protected from further harm. Also there is a chance that if you do not act quickly then your partner or spouse may get in there first. Get the balance right between making an informed decision by having fruitful discussions, but also by acting quickly.

The biggest question you need to ask yourself when making this decision is:

'Who am I and what do I want from life? How do I want my children to grow up? Is what I want feasible in my current situation?'

If you are staying together for the children, this is the worst thing you could do for them. Do you want them to witness the abuse and hostility you have been tolerating?

If you are holding back from divorce because of the reasons I have mentioned then I hope this chapter has given you some light and inner guidance.

Chapter 2 – Decision Made, The Next Step

Now that you have made your decision there are some practical considerations. These include the temporary sorting of finances, retrieving any belongings from the former matrimonial home, arrangements for the children and, most importantly, consulting a solicitor. The previous issues can be resolved better once you have instructed a solicitor.

I appreciate that many things will need resolving before you instruct a solicitor and it is better to try and get moving on these sooner rather than later. Once you have sent the petition out, everything will move very quickly and you will have to think on your feet. On top of that the fireworks with your ex will also ignite.

Communicating With Your Ex

If you still have to communicate with your ex regarding the children, for example, keep communications short and sweet, without confrontation and, most importantly, log everything. Ideally communicate by text or email to keep everything documented as things can and will be misconstrued.

Returning To The Former Matrimonial Home

If you need to return to the former matrimonial home to retrieve your belongings, take someone with you and do it while your ex is not there to avoid any incident.

However, communicate with your ex that it is your intention to return to the home.

Before you have your first consultation with a solicitor there is certain documentation that you will require. It will be a big time saver to have all this to hand before the meeting. Forward planning and quick, decisive action are a must.

Sort The Two P's: Pin Numbers And Passwords

If your ex knows any pin numbers or passwords to any email accounts etc. change them forthwith. I have seen a lot of very close friends get caught out on this one, where they have divorced and several months' later money has come out of their account that they have not spent. It turned out that the ex knew their pin number and withdrew large amounts of money from their account. If you have a joint account this is something you will need to check with your financial advisor. Fortunately in my case this was not a concern as we did not have any joint accounts.

When it comes to instructing a solicitor, think about what your needs are. For example, I had a lot issues around racism and the threat of residence and possible abduction. When I went on the website of my chosen firm, I found a lot of their solicitors had expertise in this area.

Find out also if the particular firm covers legal aid cases or publically funded cases, as many do not. The rules around legal aid are always changing; ensure you seek advice on this. Try and choose a solicitor through word of mouth or personal recommendation. In many cases the first consultation will be free.

Before your first consultation, prepare, prepare and prepare. You will need to sit down and have a good think about your grounds for divorce and write out a detailed chronology of the dates and incidents that have taken place. This is like a first draft of your divorce petition. It is time consuming and draining, and can make you very emotional. However, it is also very therapeutic and it gets you thinking more about what you want. In my case once I started writing I could not stop. The more I wrote, I kept asking myself the question, 'Why didn't I do this a long time ago?'

If you are divorcing on grounds of unreasonable behaviour this has many categories to it. A solicitor can go through the legal aspects of this but I will go through the emotional. Do not ever feel that just because your ex never raised his hand to you this does not count as abuse. Psychological and emotional abuse also counts, and many women feel they are to blame. A very close friend of mine ended up in a refuge as a result of domestic violence. In that refuge she met another young girl who was a model; her husband disapproved of her modelling career, accusing her of prostituting her body. He never laid a finger on her but this is an example of controlling behaviour. I know women who frequently listen to put downs from their husbands; such as they are ugly and they should feel obliged to their husbands for keeping a roof over their heads. Wrong! You deserve to be treated with respect and marriage is an equal partnership. You are not your husband's maid. If someone loves and cares for you they should look after you and not make you feel indebted to them. Real love is unconditional.

Also emphasise your positive points and the steps you have taken to mend the marriage such as counselling and supporting the family financially, especially if you had these sorts of troubles in your marriage.

If at the stage of putting a petition together you are still having doubts about whether you are doing the right thing or not, the stage of drafting the petitions will answer this question for you. The biggest question you will be able to answer at the end of it is, 'Has my marriage broken down irretrievably?'

Chapter 3 – At The First Consultation

With Your Solicitor

You should feel much empowered about taking this step because it is a big one. It is the step where you are making a stand and taking control of your destiny. Never underestimate the importance of what you are doing, which is standing up to bullies through legal action.

Purpose Of The First Consultation

Your first consultation is an opportunity to ask questions, iron out concerns and find out what your rights are. As well as your documentation and draft petition etc., write out a list of your concerns.

Costs Of Divorce

At this stage you should also look at whether you would qualify for legal aid or not. If you have to fund the case privately, try and find out roughly what the costs are and think about savings you have. Be aware legal aid is something which is always changing, so please check with a legal expert on this. Many public service organisations have employee assistance support with a legal department. If you work in this type of organisation it is worth looking into this advice, which often extends to debt counselling etc.

At the back of this book you will find a list of useful sites to visit for general advice around finances etc.

Dealing With Any Ongoing Issues Before Sending Out The Petition

Before even sending the petition out there are many issues that can be dealt with. If your ex is still harassing you or your family, discuss this with your solicitor. They may be able to suggest a pre-petition letter.

You will be advised about mediation and trying to resolve matters out of court. If you know that realistically this is not possible, be very frank with your solicitor about this.

You should walk away from this first consultation better informed of your rights and feeling reassured. If you do not, then this is a sign that you need another opinion. For me personally I felt very reassured and was fired up to just get the process started.

A good solicitor will fight your corner and inform you of what you can realistically expect within the boundaries of the law. However, also be aware that whoever you instruct, for them it is only a job. This case is personal to you and about your child, therefore you will need to be very proactive about pushing the outcome you require. Some solicitors want to go for an option that is easy for them, necessitating less work. Do not settle for this if it is not the right option for you or your child. Remember time is of the essence, so if you get a positive vibe from the solicitor you have seen, then proceed to the next stage, and be decisive.

Chapter 4 – Giving Your Ex Notice Of

Proceedings

As I explained in the previous chapter, before you even send the petition out, once a solicitor is involved there are ways they can immediately diffuse matters with your ex by sending out a pre-petition letter.

Setting The Boundaries

Issues such as retrieving belongings and making arrangements for the children can be addressed through your solicitor. These proceedings are between you and your ex, and your children should be the first priority. I have seen many situations where the ex-in-laws have also got involved, which is highly inappropriate. This is something you can set boundaries on in the first letter that is issued. Depending on how acrimonious the proceedings are, your solicitor is more than likely to advise that you cut all communications with your ex and communicate via your solicitor. Ensure you follow this advice to the letter and report back to your solicitor if your ex or his family do not comply. Despite a solicitor's instructions there is still a chance they will not comply, but you need to set the boundaries. Remember your ex-husband and in-laws will not like being told what to do. The shock factor will be you standing up to them. You are taking control of the situation and they will not like it and will push you and test you to the maximum. Taking this control, however, is very empowering and you will no longer feel like the victim. Just an example, I was suffering with very high blood pressure prior to and after giving birth. When I had my blood pressure checked a couple of weeks after sending the petition, my results had returned to normal.

The pre-petition letter allows you some breathing space before sending out the petition.

Putting A Draft Petition Together
Based on the chronology you provided, your solicitor will start putting the petition together. When you receive it ensure it is accurate and you have not missed anything. Once it is filed, it will become a live legal document that will be referred to during the proceedings, which is why it is imperative to ensure it is accurate.

Job Done, Sit Tight And Wait
Now that you have instructed a solicitor, sent out the first letter and the petition, it is time to let go and sit tight and wait. You should again feel empowered at your strength to take control of a situation and allow someone else, i.e. your solicitor, to deal with matters for you. This is the point where you should feel reassured and protected. Now that you have made this a legal matter your ex cannot touch you and you do not need to feel afraid of him any more. If he tries anything, you have the law on your side. The goal posts have switched and you are in control. Adopt this mantra to get you through:

'I claim my power and move beyond all limitations.'

Chapter 5 – The Aftermath: Keep Hold

Of The Remote

Once your ex has received the petition, this is when all the mud slinging and allegations can start. Remember: this is reflective of their character not yours.

Dealing With Allegations

It is highly unlikely that your ex will admit to the contents of the divorce petition. In fact you may get portrayed as the villain. For example, if you suffer from depression, this will be used against you. Threats of residence and unfit parenting allegations are what you could be looking it. This is the reality of what I experienced in my own case.

When I sent my petition out I went through months of various allegations, mud slinging and harassment of me and my family. You name it we went through it all.

I would panic, get upset and be up until all hours mulling over the correspondence received via solicitors. In my case there were also issues over my ex's representation. One minute he had a mediator, a cheap alternative to a solicitor, and the next minute he was representing himself. While I was getting upset I realised many of the emails were simply 'FYI' (for your information) emails. When my ex made the residence threat, my solicitors straightened the matter out immediately, without needing to take instructions from me. This is the beauty of having a solicitor. To this day my ex makes this threat, but now I am so immune to it that I can even laugh it off. A threat of residence is scary but that is what your ex is trying to achieve. Check with your own legal advisor but residence is changed only in very extreme cases.

The Practical Side Of Responding To Allegations

By all means read the correspondence, draft a response and instruct your solicitors. It is important to maintain a balance between dealing with the issues and not letting this dictate your life. Keep focused with the matters in hand, i.e. arrangements for the children. Despite allegations etc. never ever retaliate. This can be difficult if you suffer from depression or your ex is someone who knows how to push your buttons and tip you over the edge. It is mind games and he is looking to prove you are an unfit mother. Never give him what he wants, hold on to your remote control. When you receive threatening correspondence hit the pause button, breathe and think before giving a response. Do not make the mistake I did at the beginning of writing a response as if you are doing a university assignment. Your solicitor will not have time to read everything and what he drafts to the other side needs to be factual. I have become more au fait with this recently and it has come with experience. Your solicitor is paid to deal with these matters, you are not their paralegal. You have other things in your life, especially your children. You have come out of this situation to give you and your child a better life; do not continue to let your ex control your life.

Do Not Let It Dictate Your Life

Please refer to the last part of this book and utilise your resources to help you manage these soul-destroying emails. By all means talk to your family and friends but do not drain them and get snappy, you will drive them away. Instead, take your mind off it by asking your mum to babysit and going to the cinema with your sister for the evening.

At all times, remember your ex is used to you being a down-trodden doormat and it will hurt his ego that you have made a stand.

After six months of mud slinging, matters to do with my daughter had to be taken to court, which was only the start of a long-haul battle.

Mayapee Chowdhury

Part 2 – Chapter 6 – The Real Legal

Battle

If matters cannot be resolved amicably then unfortunately court is the only solution. This process can involve other professionals such as social services, CAFCASS and a psychologist. In some cases school and medical records have to be looked into and many professionals may wish to visit you at home. This is where the real legal battle starts; it will feel like your life is not your own any more. That is, if you let it.

In this section I will go through the different types of court hearings you may have to attend and how to prepare for them on a practical and emotional front. I will also cover how to prepare yourself for interviews with professionals and home visits.

I will guide you through how to ensure you are not intimidated by anyone and you stand your ground. When other professionals become involved you will need to strike a balance between being assertive and cooperative. As always, please remember what I am saying is for guidance only, please ensure you consult with the relevant legal professionals.

Chapter 7 – First Appointments And

Directions Hearings

When matters commence in the court arena the first hearing is called a first appointment. In my experience this is heard by a judge where interim measures will be made for contact. Matters around contact and finances are dealt with separately by the courts; an issue that can cause debate as, in my view, the two are linked. A first appointment is a directions hearing, which I will elaborate on. When your case goes to court it can be heard by a judge or magistrates.

When matters get to court there are various hearings that can take place; one type is a directions hearing. These hearings usually take place to review previous court orders and they can be listed from fifteen minutes to half an hour, although you have the whole day to negotiate. If heard by a magistrate these hearings can be more complex. Magistrates are not legally qualified or paid, what they do is a voluntary service to the community. Although they have a legal advisor on hand they are not obliged to take the advice given. Please note: if your case gets very complex it may be worth speaking to your solicitor about transferring your case to the County Court.

I have experience of both and prefer hearings heard by a judge, especially when your ex is self-represented. In the Magistrates Court, I found my ex got the sympathy vote for representing himself. During one hearing the magistrate chairing the bench would not even allow my barrister to cross-examine him properly. They can take prolonged periods just for a directions hearing.

With a judge, on the other hand, an order can be drafted beforehand merely for the judge to sign off. The legal training makes them more decisive. With my solicitor I tried for a long time to get my case transferred to the County Court, the magistrates' chair refused despite the advice of a legal advisor. Ultimately my case did get transferred. This shows how lack of legal expertise can not only cause errors but also prolong proceedings.

Again based on my own experiences, magistrates will follow a CAFCASS recommendation to the letter. This is a disadvantage if you have a CAFCASS officer who is against you and makes a recommendation that is not in your favour. After hearing from counsel, a judge on the other hand, may exercise some discretion.

Directions Hearings

A directions hearing listed in front of a judge can be more straightforward as they are legally qualified; however, be aware they take a firm hand too. Directions hearings are not about hearing evidence or going through complex statements and cross-examination. If this is required then the matter will be listed for a longer hearing. In the next chapter I will go through longer hearings. Normally the orders made in a directions hearing are by agreement, and if something is in dispute it can be listed. Directions hearings are more about looking at interim measures to tackle issues. Please note when this type of hearing is before a judge they can enforce orders. Magistrates are limited as they are not legally qualified.

Preparing For A Directions Hearing

If you want the best outcome for your child and have concerns, preparation is crucial. About a week before the hearing have a consultation with your solicitor and ensure that you are fully briefed about what the hearing is about. This is your opportunity to ask questions and put your case across to get a favourable outcome. It is worth putting together a small statement of what your concerns are, the outcome you are looking for, and why. Your solicitor can submit this statement to your barrister so that they are fully briefed before the hearing. Although your solicitor will support you, be aware they will also have to play devil's advocate and they will put to you the argument that the other party may put forward. This is your opportunity to come up with an appropriate response.

Taking Care Of Yourself When Preparing For A Hearing

The day before the hearing ensure you take time out for yourself to do some exercise and breathing, whatever puts you in a calm state of mind. Although it is a directions hearing, there can be a lot of waiting around and it is not always easy to get access to canteen facilities. Ensure you get a good night's sleep, and on the day be fully nourished.

The Day Itself

You will be required to arrive at least an hour before the hearing to negotiate with the other side. This is also an opportunity for you to have a pre-case conference with your barrister. If you have given your solicitor a statement beforehand this is where that will come in useful. Once in that situation it becomes very stressful, therefore it is better to be prepared beforehand. Time is limited in a pre-case conference and your barrister will also have to negotiate with the other side and other agencies involved.

Drafting Orders In Court

If there is anything specific you would like drafted in a court order, mention this before going in front of a magistrate or judge. For example, if contact is for the father only, that can be worded in the court order. I have seen situations where the contact application is for the father only but they take it upon themselves to bring their whole family, new girlfriend etc. If there is no communication between you and your ex, then consider using a contact book, this can also be included in the order. Be very clear about contact times, handover arrangements, lateness, dates etc. If you know in advance that there are days you are not available, make this known to the Court. The court order is a legally binding document and if any non-compliance takes place you can refer back to it. You have control over what is put in it.

If You Are Not Satisfied With The Outcome

If you walk away from a hearing dissatisfied with the outcome, take some time out to reflect. One thing I have learnt is that orders are made in Court and the situation can change like the weather. For example, my solicitors and I spent a whole morning negotiating in Court only for my ex to phone them later on to say he would not be attending contact. Orders made at directions hearings are seldom final orders and if there are problems along the way there may be provision to take matters back to Court. Remember, a directions hearing is about finding an interim solution to a problem. Within that order your ex may have to undertake a vast amount of work. Sit back and watch to see whether he can rise to the challenge or not.

Chapter 8 – The Longer Hearings:

Preparation, Preparation, Preparation!

These are often called fact-finding hearings or contested hearings. They can last anything from a full day to three days. I cannot reiterate this enough: preparation is crucial. Be proactive when it comes to putting statements and other supporting evidence together, and keep a log of incidents. If you have any incident numbers etc., ensure they are in a safe place and ready to be submitted as evidence. Preparation for this type of hearing will certainly need one, maybe two face-to-face consultations with your solicitor. Although you will meet your barrister on the day of the hearing, it will be a stressful day. Preparation can make a huge difference to the outcome.

The Months Leading Up To The Hearing

It is more than likely that you will be given several months' notice of this hearing. Do not spend these months brooding. You will need to find the right balance between living your life and enjoying all daily activities, and also getting ready for the hearing. By all means rally support and confide in people, but be selective about this. Remember it may be difficult for people to empathise with you if they do not have enough life experience. Please refer to the final section of the book regarding sources of support.

Leading A Normal Life

Trying to lead a normal life is also part of psyching yourself up to delivering your best on the day. Think of all the positive aspects of your present life and enjoy them to the full. It will manifest itself in how you come across in front of your ex. For example, the night before one particular hearing I gave a performance of my poetry at a prestigious venue in Leicester. My performance was very well received and I made some vital contacts. I went into Court on a high with a confidence boast. When I had allegations thrown at me, I reflected back to the previous night on stage. Along with preparing for this hearing and looking after my daughter, I had also been taking part in intensive but enjoyable rehearsals for this performance. This is what I mean about the importance of balance.

The energy or vibes you send out to the other side is also crucial. I have seen a big difference in outcomes when I present in a nervous shaky demeanour as opposed to a positive, happy, glowing manner. The latter makes my ex fall apart without even trying. It may sound like a cliché but actions are stronger than words.

The Big Day

The day of the hearing will feel unending. You may come face to face with witnesses for the other side. For example, my ex-in-laws were called in as witnesses for one hearing. They had smug looks on their faces and it brought back painful memories. My solicitor kept nudging me and saying, 'Stop looking at them.' She was absolutely right, be poker faced and look confident.

To date the hearing with my ex-in-laws present was the longest and most draining day of my life. However, I also got a positive outcome due to my overall presence and attitude, and I barely spoke at that hearing. I put on a new shiny suit, high heels, got myself a stylish haircut, and wore the most self-confidence ever. Without saying very much, the hearing went in my favour. The old expression, 'silence is the best weapon' is so true.

The best advice I have been given is by a very dear friend who is a boxer:

'It is not about fighting harder, but smarter, and knowing your opponent's weaknesses.'

Fighting Tactics
My solicitor sussed out quickly that the calmer I remained, the harder my ex had to try to make me react and that was when he would lose it. This is what I mean by getting a verdict in my favour without doing anything.

Remember at all times, your ex knows which of your buttons to push, so keep hold of your remote.

It is difficult to prepare for actual cross-examination and giving evidence from a practical point of view. In any breaks that you have, take the opportunity to do some breathing exercises and draw upon any affirmations or mantras that keep you strong.

The other side will definitely find ways of trying to brand you as unstable and painting your ex as the victim; stay firm and calm. Staying calm and confident will get you through. If your ex is representing himself, he will have to cross-examine you. This can be very intimidating and it is easy to react. It is better to let him hang himself by making himself look like a fool. My solicitor kept telling me:

'The calmer you remain, the harder he has to try to provoke you.'

Chapter 9 – Difficult Interviews

At various stages of the process you may have to undergo difficult interviews, sometimes with your ex present. These can be with CAFCASS or a psychologist. Sometimes they may visit you at home and sometimes in their office. There may be instances when your ex also needs to be present. However, if there are issues of domestic violence you can request to be seen separately.

<u>Your First Meeting With A CAFCASS Officer</u>
The very first experience I had of seeing a CAFCASS officer on my own was a nightmare and resulted in me making a complaint. This was at the early stages of my case when I was still getting my head around the system. A disadvantage I faced, which can be common, is that this officer had a meeting with my ex the very same morning and had already formed an opinion. That should not be the case but it does happen. An officer with experience and common sense will handle this situation in a sensitive manner. If, however, this is not the case, you can take control of the meeting. Insist as much as possible for you to be seen individually. There may be situations when this is unavoidable, for example if your child's school is involved. Try to speak to whomever may be chairing the meeting beforehand to express your concerns. An experienced officer, however, should handle a meeting with sensitivity. For example, there is provision for you to stagger your and your ex's arrival

and departure times and be seated in separate waiting areas. You may also be allowed to have someone present, such as a family member or friend, for moral support. Always check on this first, though, as there could be an issue around confidentiality.

If The Meeting Is Not Going Your Way
In these one-to-one situations especially, do not commit yourself to anything you are not happy with. You are not in court of law but you will be made to feel like you are. It is your right to consult with a solicitor if you are not happy to commit to something. If you are asked to divulge information you are not happy with; again, before committing, speak to your solicitor.

The interview you have will not be confidential; anything you say will go back to your ex and more than likely the courts. My message is do not discuss anything if you do not want it to be repeated. You are being watched and judged in these interviews, therefore err on the side of caution in what you divulge about yourself. This really is a situation where you have to engage your brain before your mouth. Anything you say can and will be misconstrued.

If you are not happy about the way a meeting is conducted, express this to the person carrying out the meeting, and after the meeting ensure you log it with your solicitor.

An Interview With A Psychologist
An interview with a psychologist can be very lengthy, intense and gruelling. Your body language will be observed, the way you dress, your punctuality,

everything, so be on top of the things you can control. Stay firm but calm, you will be made to feel like you are in the wrong.

For example, if you tell a psychologist that your ex abused you by doing X, Y and Z, the response you may get is, 'How is that abuse?" Remember, the experience was yours; stand your ground and do not let anyone undervalue your feelings in these matters.

At the end of the day, for a psychologist or CAFCASS officer this is a job and will not affect them by five o'clock in the evening. For you, it is your life and, most importantly, your child's life. *You* have lived through the traumas, not them. Never feel you are inferior to these people because far from it, you are not. A psychologist is only educated about life experience by a degree. The unfortunate thing is they may have been directed by CAFCASS to approach the interview in a certain way, therefore having already formed an opinion. Just to give an example: if a CAFCASS officer or guardian is determined that contact should progress to overnight stays and they feel you are an obstructive mother, the officer has the power to steer the psychologist in such a way that they make that finding about you. I have learnt this from experience. Unfortunately with activist groups such as the Justice for Fathers movement, mothers are often accused of being obstructive. It is how you come across. I unfortunately did not come across in a positive way following the psychologist's assessment. Now I am working hard to redeem myself. Based on my own experiences, I strongly recommend some sort of coaching and preparation from an expert such as a counsellor or, if you have access, an independent psychologist. A report made by a psychologist carries weight as they have credentials coming out of their ears. They are likely to have read background information and delved into your medical and employment history etc., which will affect their write up.

Although it is possible to turn things around if the report is not in your favour, it is difficult. Please refer to the final part of the book to keep yourself in the best mental and physical health to stay ahead of the game.

Following the interview the interviewer will interpret the information how they want to, you do not have to agree with the report that has been written. In part three I will go through what to do if you are not happy.

Chapter 10 – Home Visits

I have experienced both the positive and negative sides of social services and CAFCASS during home visits. Many factors can affect this:

<u>Your Attitude</u>
You can look at this in two ways: very intrusive, with people barging into your home playing God, or you can embrace it and look at it as your opportunity to shine. This is your manifestation of the new life you have created: an independent woman who can juggle a child, career and the domestic responsibilities of running a home. It is probably something that your ex believed you were not capable of. Maybe your life has improved since your ex has been out of your life. This is your opportunity to prove it. The effort is worth it and a big tick in your favour.

<u>Making Your House Spic And Span</u>
Take the time to make your house beautiful, enlist the support of family and friends. Make it look homely and child friendly. Health and safety is an area to give special attention to. I know someone who got slated for leaving mail on the stairs. When I have watched programmes such as *Panorama* and *Dispatches,* I have seen extremely unhygienic living conditions with excrement on the floor and no bedding on the bed.

Be extra cautious on the hygiene front in particular. It is often the case that an officer will use your bathroom, not because they necessarily need it, but to again check on living conditions. All officers are different. One officer made an unannounced visit and commented on clutter and the fact that my daughter had drawn on the wall. I have seen this in two-parent families as well. However, another officer saw my flat in a similar condition and made positive remarks. It often depends on who you get. As I have become more experienced in these proceedings I have found ways of winning people round.

Be Welcoming

When they arrive, be very welcoming; offer refreshments and keep all the room doors open to show that you have nothing to hide. Your child's room will be the pièce de résistance of the visit. It is more than likely that whoever comes out to see you will want to see your child's room, but if they do not it goes in your favour to volunteer it.

Having somebody visiting you can be an invasion of privacy and very nerve racking (please utilise the last section of the book on how to cope with this), but you can request that a family member is present. Although organisations such as social services have powers to make unannounced visits etc., you also have rights. They should also try to work round your child's routine and your work commitments. Stress to them the importance of you keeping on top of your job to provide for your child and the importance of your child not being disrupted in school hours. If they do activities out of school which you have paid for, stress that you are a single mother who cannot throw money down the drain.

Always remember you are not inferior to these people and there is no need to feel intimidated by anyone. You will need to get the balance right between being cooperative and accommodating, but also assertive, tactful and not being a pushover. There have been instances when home visits have clashed with my daughter's activities and my own work commitments. Be honest and open about this; you have a life and your kids are entitled to one, these people do not rule your life. Social services are very manipulative and will want to carry out visits according to their convenience. If you do not make yourself available you will be accused of being uncooperative and a neglectful mother etc. Keep lines of communication open and always return calls, which will minimise your stress levels. You should take the lead in obtaining mobile numbers and email addresses etc., in fact all lines of communication with a social worker. That way if you cannot return a phone call, for example, then you have another means of communication and cannot be accused of being uncooperative. My experiences of social services have been both negative and positive. One social worker only gave an office landline as a contact number and the line was always busy. When I could not return calls etc. she would make unannounced visits and lecture me about how my daughter comes first. Since then I have learned my lesson and keep several numbers handy and always at least try to text an officer if I am unable to take their call. NEVER ignore their calls; this causes more suspicion.

Never feel inferior to these people; if anything you are likely to be the complete opposite to them. Many officers

I have come across do not have children themselves, and have less education and life experience than I do.

All these officers in power have tried very hard to brand me as mentally ill, and I admit that on a couple of occasions I have lost my cool and had an outburst. This is not an ideal situation to get into, but if it happens then apologise and take responsibility; you are only human and cannot be a saint all of the time.

Social services have a lot of power; however, so do you. It is about getting a good balance between being cooperative, assertive and leading a normal life. I will be the first to say this is not easy and can often feel impossible.

The powers of social services extend as far as care orders. This is where they can actually take parental responsibility of your child and override any decisions you make. You can stay in control of this. If you cooperate, keep lines of communications open and engage with offers of help they will be happy and will eventually limit their involvement. It is frustrating; however, the bigger picture for you is to keep residence of your child.

In the next part of this handbook I will talk about social media. Without trying to scare anyone, social services have targets around taking children into care etc. If you cooperate and engage with them you can take control of how much power they have over your child.

Part 3 – When Things Do Not Go Your Way

All is not lost if things do not go your way, there are other avenues you can explore. In this section I will go through these with you.

I will try to point you in the right direction if putting in a complaint against an organisation or accessing your MP. Based on some of my own experiences, I will try to guide you through how to formulate letters of complaint.

Your solicitor is your first port of call when you are not happy, I will also go through how to put a statement together if you disagree with a report that has been made.

I will also talk about networking and social media to help your case. Knowledge is power and if you come across people who have been through similar experiences to you, this can help you a great deal.

Chapter 11 – Complaints Procedures

If you believe you have been treated in an unfair manner by an organisation such as CAFCASS, then explore their complaints procedure. You will need to go on to the CAFCASS website to explore their internal procedures. Please check the back of this book for links to useful websites, including this link.

Trying To Resolve Matters Informally Via The Organisation

Each local office has their own internal route. Within any organisation there is a level of discretion that can be exercised. Not all my experiences of CAFCASS have been negative. There was one CAFCASS service manager who actually had a meeting with me about my concerns and operated in a co-worker capacity with the CAFCASS officer that I was unhappy with. The services manager also supervised some contact and sat in on meetings between myself and the CAFCASS officer. This is a lucky and rare situation where I had someone who was prepared to go beyond the tick box and go the extra mile.

Making A Complaint

Many aspects of any complaint you have may need to be raised in Court as CAFCASS officers and guardians are usually appointed by the Court. Before taking matters further, you will need to start by writing to your local

CAFCASS services manager. Always check the CAFCASS website as these policies and procedures are subject to change.

Be very careful in the tactics you adopt when making your complaint. It is worth getting your solicitor to check your letter before sending it off. Many mothers at the moment are being accused of being obstructive and complaining for the sake of it. Make sure your complaint cannot be misinterpreted as malice. Keep it factual and illustrate specific examples that can be backed up. It may be worth considering any supporting evidence that you may have to strengthen your case. If you feel you have been spoken to inappropriately or rudely, this is a point for complaint. For example, I had a CAFCASS officer who used hand gestures to stop me from talking and she apologised for doing so.

If you feel you have been treated in a biased manner and your voice has not been heard, put it in your letter of complaint. A good CAFCASS officer will listen to both sides and put the needs of the child first without any bias towards either parent.

Another situation I faced was when a CAFCASS guardian kept calling me at work, insisting on speaking to me. These proceedings are confidential and I work in a public facing office. I made this point clear in the complaint, got an apology, and the officer never did this again. It may not seem like it, but making a complaint can have even a small impact on a situation.

There are a high number of complaints against CAFCASS and it is well publicised in the media that social services are making mistakes and children are suffering. There are issues around heavy workloads and lack of training. By putting in a complaint you could be flagging up these issues and possibly impacting on reform. Never feel that complaining is pointless because you never know what is going on behind closed doors.

The Next Stage If You Are Still Unhappy

If you are not happy with the outcome of your complaint via the internal procedure, look at taking it to the next stage, which is the ombudsman. The ombudsman can be accessed via your local MP, and there are many flaws in the system as a whole, which could also be worth highlighting by writing to your local MP. They may not be able to interfere in existing proceedings but your views could lead to some reform in the system.

If a complaint is taken to this stage you will need to show that all local resolution options have been explored. When making this complaint you will need to emphasise how you or your child have been impacted. Please be aware that the ombudsman may ask for the matter to be referred back to CAFCASS if they feel they have not looked into the matter properly.

Another note of caution is that the ombudsman may not feel it is serious enough for them to take the case at all.

In my own case, many matters worked themselves out through the involvement of other professionals, therefore I chose not to pursue this avenue.

Chapter 12 – What Happens When You Disagree With A Report Or Recommendation?

In reports you may be portrayed in a negative light and what you say may be misconstrued. If you strongly disagree with something, make it known. Often saying nothing can be taken as acceptance of what has been said. You have the right to have your say in any recommendations about your child's future, as well as the right to defend yourself against any allegations.

As I explained in the previous chapter, many issues that you may have with CAFCASS or social services can be explored in Court by looking at statements, further evidence and cross examination.

When you read a report, the first reading may upset you and it may not be the best time to make a decision. Go back to it fresh after a few days and consider getting a more neutral second reader to take a look at it. Highlight what you disagree with and why, giving your defences, and correcting inaccuracies and misrepresentations. Put your points together and submit them to your solicitor who can use them to put a statement together. If you have further evidence to back up what you are saying, bring it to your solicitor's attention.

Also consider areas you could improve on. If, for example, you suffer from depression, seek therapy if it is advised. It looks better to be proactive. Sometimes the negative points made about you can be turned around into a positive, and looked at differently.

The Findings Of A Psychological Assessment

I am still getting over the psychological assessment made about me, although it is possible to take control of proving the professionals wrong. Despite having favourable reports and a CAFCASS officer onside, I have seen situations where the other party cannot live up to them. Following the report, if other professionals are brought in, get these people on your side and re-evaluate your strategy.

Remember CAFCASS merely advise and make recommendations to the Court; it is the judge who will make the final decisions. It is possible for the Court to make a ruling contrary to the CAFCASS recommendation. This has happened to me on several occasions. Also there are points on a recommendation that you may be able to negotiate on or reach a compromise on. This is where networking with other people can help, which leads into the next chapter.

Recently I was in a situation when CAFCASS and social services etc. were all against me and branded me as mentally unstable. When it got to Court the judge supported me and I got an outcome in my favour, contrary to the CAFCASS recommendations. It is more than possible that, as in boxing, knowing your opponent's weakness will help you fight accordingly.

Chapter 13 – Networking And Making Social Media Work For You – Knowledge Is Power

Knowledge is power. Many positives have come out of my situation and one is the friends I have made during my journey. I have taken my daughter to contact centres for supervised contact and attended a parenting information programme. At both of these I not only made some meaningful friendships, I also learned I was not alone.

You can all be a support for each other and bounce ideas off each other. There may be some technique that is being used in someone else's case that you could also suggest to your solicitor and vice versa. One thing that inspired me to write this book is how so many people are not aware of their rights. Social services and CAFCASS can put the fear of God in anyone. People want to complain but do not know how. You can also pick up a lot of insider knowledge on mistakes that have been made. This can fire you up to fight smarter; it is easy to give in and think, *What's the point?* It is also easy to take matters personally and feel low about yourself. When you find out someone else is going through what you are going through, or worse, you can support one another.

I have also made friends with other women in similar situations at work, my daughter's school, and social activities. I am also good friends with some social workers (I stress they have never been involved in my case) and picked up insider knowledge, for example around pro-fathering. Organisations are under the deluded impressions that the maternal side poisons and influences children against fathers and that is why CAFCASS are in a position where they feel they should allow contact to fathers at whatever cost. I would not know this if I were not sociable; knowledge is power. When armed with knowledge like this you do not feel intimidated by CAFCASS.

Many MPs and organisations within these proceedings have a Twitter page. This is useful to generally express your views about the family court system.

The various anti-social-services and CAFCASS complaints on Facebook and Twitter will also show you how knowledge is power and again you can rally your own network via this route. However, please make your solicitor aware of what you are doing. Never name any parties in the proceedings, especially judges or CAFCASS officers; you could be in contempt of Court. From social media you will again find you are not alone and that you are not a troublemaker. These campaigns exist because of people like us who are suffering. They also show the mistakes that these organisations are making and how we are right to fight our cause and never give up.

Before a meeting, home visit or court case, it can be very empowering to walk in with insider knowledge which you can only get by networking. In a very diplomatic manner, when you are made to feel powerless you can intelligently throw this knowledge back in the face of a CAFCASS officer or social services. For example when I have been told that my ex-in-laws are very lovely people the reaction I have often given is, 'So was Baby P's mother.' You can often plant a seed to make people think. When they find out you are a sociable person with self awareness they will know they cannot easily bully you. I repeat:

Knowledge is power!

Part 4 – Look After Yourself

The final part of the book I feel is a crucial part, with tips on looking after yourself. You may ask the question why this is not the beginning of the book. I am of the belief that in order to know how to look after yourself you need to know what you have ahead of you. It is similar to when a maintenance guy comes out to do a repair. There is a chance he or she will look at what has been damaged and then consider the tools and work required to repair the damage. This last part is really about the emotional, social and spiritual toolbox you need to survive this ordeal.

I will give you my own personal tips on looking after yourself physically and emotionally, how to balance the relationships around you, and how to have a healthy and fulfilled career and social life. I promise you these things are possible during such soul-destroying proceedings; living proof is all around me and I have also done it myself.

Chapter 14 – Looking After Your Health

Your Health Is Your Wealth.

During these proceedings there will be upsets in your routine and constant disruptions, and you will have to think on your feet. The court proceedings alone can be detrimental to your respiratory system. As I said earlier, my character has taken a battering and I still live to tell the tale. I am learning how to take control of the situation, not the other way round. I appreciate it is difficult; I am still on a journey myself.

During my journey I have drawn from various sources of strength that have kept me sane and functioning. These include yoga, meditation, affirmations, chanting, breathing, crystal healing etc. Sometimes you may have to go through trial and error to find what works for you. The good thing is these are all natural and holistic ways of healing, but a godsend when your system is knocked out of balance during a court hearing.

There is no shame in going to your GP and having counselling, and even taking medication if you need it. You would need to be a saint to keep your sanity during the stress of these proceedings. For a while I resisted visiting my GP and asking for help in case it went against me in front of my ex. I was wrong, the opposite can happen. You need to stay mentally, physically, emotionally and spirituality healthy in this game. Your ex, his family and the organisations will try to break you and grind you down. Your overall health and wellbeing will save you, and you also need all round wellbeing for your children. You will see from previous chapters that you do not have just one battle but other mini-battles, and on top of this a child to look after, a job, and a home to run.

When the various assessments made about me emphasised my depression, I took the advice and support I was offered on board. There is no shame in being open and putting your hands up to it. Trying to conceal it causes more problems, but do not let anyone make you feel incapable of it.

Depression is as common as having a cold nowadays, even very successful people have battled with it. Emphasise to the authorities that you are dealing with it, as well as all your good points. I openly admit I suffer with depression but I am by no means incapable. I am holding down a job, a decent pace to stay, and have an abundance of talents where I have achieved.

These proceedings take over your life, on top of that you have to raise a child. Never be hard on yourself if you break down, it is a sign you are human and have reached your limits.

It is easy to give up, give in and say, 'What's the point?' I have seen the difference for myself. Whenever I have taken the 'what's the point' mentality, everything has fallen apart and gone negatively for me.

When I have kept a balance of eating right, taking regular exercise, looking after my spiritual health, and other positives in my life, I have sent out a positive vibe to those around me and good results have come almost effortlessly. You cannot physically attack a judge or

CAFCASS officer even though you may want to. Your overall wellbeing is the biggest weapon you have.

Chapter 15 – Balancing These

Proceedings With A Successful Career

I strongly advocate being a working mum and you should never feel guilty about that. You are providing for your child, instilling a strong work ethic in them, and maybe even starting a legacy or empire that they could take over one day.

Do not put any of your dreams and aspirations on hold because of your legal battle. It is easy to say, for example, 'I'll wait until my case is over before I start a business.' Your case could drag on for up to ten years, that's ten years of your life plus the years you may have lost when you were married.

I know women whose divorces have been the making of them. I do not claim to be perfect, but my own life is definitely better without my ex. During my legal battle I completed a postgraduate degree and pursued my writing career more actively. I published two e-books, started a blog, joined a writers' group and got back into performance poetry. Although I enjoy my day job, I would like writing to ultimately be my career. These are opportunities that I could not even dream of when I was married. I try to surround myself with women who have achieved, despite going through a legal battle.

If you are working for an employer, make sure you handle the situation diplomatically at work. Fortunately I work for an organisation that advocates work/life balance and has policies and procedures around leave for Court and other appointments. Keep your employer onside and be a model employee so that your employer does not begrudge you taking time off. If you have to take time off then make it up to your employer by putting in extra hours, for example.

This is where you will need to be assertive with organisations like CAFCASS. It is not always possible to have control over court dates, but it is not unreasonable to ask for any other appointments to fit in with your work commitments. Part of parental responsibility is being able to provide for your child by earning a living, therefore it is not reasonable to expect you to keep taking short-notice time off where it can be avoided.

Your HR department and organisations such as ACAS can give you some guidance on how to manage a situation like this at work. If you are a member of a trade union it is also worth speaking to your local representative.

Chapter 16 – Your Social Life: Avoiding

Faux Amis And FAG's

This period in your life will certainly teach you something about friendship, you really find out who your true friends are. Throughout this turbulent time in your life you need friends who will support you, uplift you when you are down, and not judge you or encroach on your privacy. It is good to get advice from other people and chat things through, but be careful about whom you trust and take advice from. I have come up with my totally non-derogatory acronym of FAG, which is a Free Advice Giver. Unless someone has walked a mile in your shoes and gone through what you have been through, they will never comprehend your situation. I would say that does not qualify them to give you advice.

As I said earlier, one of the best things that have come out of my situation is the new people that have come into my life. The whole process has been detoxifying as not only have I got rid of a negative relationship, but I have also been forced to purge some toxic friends. Although I have an abundance of support from family and friends now, it has not always been that way. Many people who I knew from childhood cut me off when they heard about all this; some people even took it as an opportunity to mock, not just me, but my family too. As harsh as it may sound, nobody is indispensable in your life and there is no void in my life as a result of these people no longer being around. It has opened up my door to more positive and spiritual friendships.

A healthy social life can make a big difference in how you deal with matters. I went through a phase when I shut myself off from everyone, which made me more depressed. Going to the cinema or for coffee with a friend can be very refreshing. My writers' group has not just been about my writing, but I have also met some very inspiring people. When I walk in I am often flustered with my mind going at one thousand miles an hour. After the writers' group I feel I have taken something better than Prozac.

The person who is, however, the biggest best friend or worst enemy in your life is you. Surround yourself with a handful of friends, but also learn to stand on your own two feet and enjoy your own company. This can be a journey of discovery for you, which leads me into the next chapter about how you present yourself.

Chapter 17 – The Power Of Dressing

The night before a court hearing or social services visit, you may be drained, having hardly slept the night before. Do not let it show on your face and never give off a slovenly vibe in how you dress and present yourself. This is again something you can do to be kind to yourself. Before a big hearing invest in a decent fitted suit and some killer heels. Take the time to get your hair done and have some DIY or salon beauty treatments to make you look and feel glowing. When you wear your killer outfit hold yourself with poise; the heels will not just lift your height but also your confidence.

For Court you will have to stick to colours like black and grey, but it does not have to be boring. During other interviews and home visits you can afford to splash a bit of colour, which can make you feel instantly revitalised. It is also very empowering when you look more pristine than some of the professionals.

Leading Up To Any Hearing
If your life has been spent in a positive way with a fulfilled job, great friends, and a healthy body and mind you have worked on, this is your chance to show off all that hard work. You will give out a strong message to your ex that despite how much he has tried to crush you, you are still standing firm. The old expression 'actions speak louder than words' has truth in it. The vibe you

send out to the professionals can also impact your case without you saying anything.

Even in terms of how you look, your divorce can make your style. If you were previously a downtrodden, controlled wife who never bothered about her looks, this is a chance to discover a new gorgeous you on that front too. You will look in the mirror and not see a trace of that downtrodden wife. The way you carry yourself will impact not just on the case but other areas of your life. The way you look and feel inside can open up new possibilities in friendships and your career. This is one area to never neglect. Even if you are feeling rubbish, just putting on a bit of lippy can make all the difference in the world. This inner calm and confidence will also affect the pace at which you speak and your overall delivery. You are being watched, judged and scrutinised. Embrace it and treat it like a performance by putting on a great show.

I am aware this is not a game; however, as I said previously, this case could suck up years of your life. You have to take control of how you cope with it, not the other way round.

A Final Word

After reading this book, if at least a couple of words of wisdom, a sentence or a whole chapter or more have influenced you, I feel I have done my job. My inspiration for this book came from seeing a gap in the market for guidance around how to deal with the practical and emotional side of divorce.

Everything I know about my rights has come from finding out for myself. When I meet other mothers in similar situations, I am shocked to find out how many of them feel they do not have any rights. They accept what is said to them because they do not know any better.

I also get asked a few questions such as: 'Can you even complain about CAFCASS?' and 'How do you complain about them?' I hope I have not only answered some of these questions, but given you a beam of light during what can be a very dark period.

I hope from reading this book you feel empowered and inspired to improve your life. Whatever stage you are at; whether you are still making the decision, are new to the system, or have an ongoing battle, I hope you have found both comfort and guidance from my personal experiences that I have shared with you.

I wrote this book for so many reasons, and I would be lying if I said I did not write it for myself. I have enjoyed sharing the journey I have been on and it has been a very therapeutic outlet for me. It is also my gift to my family and friends who have supported me throughout my journey. This is the strength that has allowed me to even contemplate writing this book. I wish this for all my readers, that you have equilibrium in your life and always stand firm for what you believe in.

God bless you all.

Useful Contacts

CAFCASS: www.cafcass.gov.uk

Ombudsman (when taking your complaint to the next stage): www.ombudsman.org.uk

Direct Gov (for benefits and debt advice): https://www.gov.uk

To locate your MP: findyourmp.parliament.uk/find.

Contacting your MP- www.parliament.uk

ACAS (for work related issues/legislation) www.acas.org.uk.